Dr. Lev G. Amusin, Ph.D.

DISSOLUTION OF GASES IN LIQUIDS AND THE FORMATION OF DISPERSION SYSTEMS IN THE MODE OF TORSION-ORIENTED TURBULIZATION

2022

DISSOLUTION OF GASES IN LIQUIDS AND THE FORMATION OF DISPERSION SYSTEMS IN THE MODE OF TORSION-ORIENTED TURBULIZATION

iUniverse books may be ordered through booksellers or by contacting:

iUniverse
1663 Liberty Drive
Bloomington, IN 47403
www.iuniverse.com
844-349-9409

ISBN: 978-1-6632-4185-6 (sc)
ISBN: 978-1-6632-4186-3 (e)

Print information available on the last page.

iUniverse rev. date: 07/11/2022

The purpose of this work is to develop the theoretical background of innovative breakthrough physicochemical processes of the dissolution of hazardous and toxic gases and the formation of dispersion systems in the mode of torsion-oriented turbulization. The phenomena in question occur in a chemical reactor installed on the vibration machine's mobile platform loaded with components of the processed dispersion system. When the external vibrational indignant forces reach certain critical parameters, the subject phenomena occur as the result of simultaneous and joint actions of mechanical resonance and fluid shock impact. Through the explosion-like action, the mixture components fill the reactor's internal chamber and convert into dispersion systems.

1. Science – Monograph – Applied Physicochemical Technology

CONTENTS

ABSTRACT

The purpose of this work is to conduct an analysis of torsion-oriented turbulization from the view of physical chemistry. The considered phenomenon in discrete and continuous modes offers breakthrough technological methods for the dissolution of gases into liquid and processing dispersion systems. One among many possible applications is process of the prevention of hazardous and toxic gas emissions into the environment by the dissolution of subject gases in compatible liquids. This is an extremely promising direction in the development of the process of chemical technology using the powerful energy of vibration.

The torsion-oriented turbulization phenomenon occurs in a chemical reactor with a chamber that has a single-cavity hyperbolic shape. The subject reactor is installed on a vibration machine, which forms a rigid mechanical vibrator–reactor system [1–5]. The reactor, with components results in the dispersion systems loaded into the reactor's chamber, being exposed to the indignant influence of a force field at accelerations of 20 to 50 times greater than that of usual terrestrial gravity acceleration. When the frequency of the indignant oscillations from the vibration machine approaches the frequency of the natural oscillations of the loaded chemical mixture, in the mixture develops mechanical resonance develops in the mixture that is followed by the fluid hammer impacts. Shock waves are extending throughout the internal volume of the reactor and lead to the violation of the dispersion medium's continuity and to the explosion-like occurrence of gas bubbles.

When the quantity of bubbles reaches a critical amount, associations of bubbles form within the processing mixture. Bubbles rotate around the vertical axel of the reactor and move upward, forming a configuration resembling the plaits of a tornado funnel. The chaotic effect of numerous bubbles on the components of the mixture causes extensive agitation that forms a dispersion system. This phenomenon is called torsion-oriented turbulization.

This phenomenon differs from known processes in its development of a uniquely large separation surface between phases that creates new technological capabilities.

INTRODUCTION

Existing methods of physicochemical technology applicable to the dissolving gases in liquid and the formation of homogeneous and heterogeneous materials have already been developed to a high degree of perfection. The further improvement of any processing technologies based on the use of additional energy, is limited and any attempts to improve the existing physicochemical processing methods are impossible in principle.

The existing technological methods of dissolving gases into the liquid and processing dispersion systems primarily are use mixers and blenders comprised of blades of different shapes placed inside chemical reactors. This design creates for contamination problems and makes processing equipment difficult to clean and disinfect. The equipment for realizing the technology under study has no moving parts, which makes this process an ideal for processing dispersion systems and chemical solutions. An additional positive side of the offered vibrational technology is its low energy consumption through the combine action of mechanical resonance and hydraulic hammer impacts.

The extremely important characteristic of the torsion-oriented turbulization is the development of an exceptionally large surface of separation between phases. Considering that all chemical reactions and physicochemical processes, including mass transfer and heat exchange, happen mainly at the surface of phase separation, this technique opens new opportunities for producing solutions and forming macro-, micro-, and nano-dispersion systems. One of the many applications is designing a process for the prevention of hazardous and toxic gas emissions [6].

In the surrounding material world, there are existing fields of power of various natures. These forces are determined by their corresponding characteristics: mechanical (e.g., gravitational), physical and mechanical (e.g., friction), physical (e.g., thermal and electromagnetic), physicochemical (e.g., molecular-surface forces) and, finally, chemical (e.g., interatomic interaction) [7]. The first three of these forces can be perceived by the human senses or by devices (gravitational, friction, thermal, and electromagnetic). These forces can interact with one another, producing the work. Forces of a physicochemical and chemical nature, however, are determined by using special methods and instruments. In addition, these forces can act on the crushed particles of solid matter and interactions between molecules and atoms to create new substances and compounds that do not exist in nature.

Torsion-orientated turbulization, considered a fundamentally new process of physicochemical technology, is based on the powerful energy of vibration [1–6]. It differs from other physicochemical processes in its unique ability to develop a substance with an exceptionally large separation surface between phases. This is important because in the dissolved gases and processed dispersion system, particles of solid matter (in suspensions) or droplets of liquid that are immiscible and insoluble in other liquids that form a dispersion phase (in emulsions) are extremely small, which triggers an increase in the influence of molecular—surface forces that, in turn, leads to a significant minimization of the dispersed phase. Thus, the offered technology enables to process dispersion systems with improved quality and extends shelf life of the final products.

In general, all dispersion systems consist of two or more components. If no collateral reversible chemical reactions are happening during the formation of such systems, then the number of components is equal to the number of substances that make up the system. If these systems form with irreversible chemical side reactions, the number of system components is equal to the difference between the number of parts that make up the system and the number of independent reactions.

Dispersion systems are considered to be two- or three-phase systems. They can be classified as follows:

Dispersion Environment	Dispersed Phase	Common Description
Gas	Liquid Droplets	Aerosol, Mist, Fog
Gas	Solid Particles	Smoke, Aerosol
Liquid	Gas	Foam
Liquid	Liquid Droplets	Emulsion*⁾
Liquid	Solid Particles	Suspension, Colloidal Solution
Solid Particles	Gas	Solid Foam
Solid Particles	Liquid	Solid Emulsion, Gel, Paste
Solid Particles	Solid Particles	Alloy, Powder

Note: *⁾ Emulsions are dispersions systems formed by minimized drops of immiscible and insoluble liquids and the dispersion medium in which they are embedded.

Dispersion systems and solutions forms as the result of the action of molecular—surface phenomena caused by the influence of the fields of external forces. During the formation of the dispersion systems the solid particles, droplets of liquid, or gas bubbles of the dispersed phase are distributed in the dispersion medium in which they are embedded. The interaction of the components of a dispersed phase and the dispersion medium defines the formation process, stability and rheological characteristics of dispersion systems.

Nanoemulsions and nanosuspensions are dispersion systems that occur during the interaction of molecular—surface force fields, which interact with particles of solid matter and liquid droplets sized 10^{-6} to 10^{-8} meters. Those compounds have special properties that are important for the effectiveness of medications taken by patients and contain important organoleptic characteristics such as cosmetic creams, pastes, and special coatings, etc.

The criterion for the similarity of the motion of heterogeneous dispersion systems is the Froude criterion (**Fr**), which can be used in cases where the influence of external disturbing forces is significant. The Froude number characterizes the ratio between the inertia force and the external force in the field in which a movement occurs, acting on the elementary volume of components of dispersion systems:

$$\boldsymbol{Fr} = \frac{\omega^2_{flow}}{gL},$$

where w_{flow} is the speed of the flow, [m/s]; g is the acceleration characterizing the action of external (gravity) force. the gravity acceleration, [9.8 m/s^2]; and L is the size of the area in which the flow is considered.

The considered physicochemical processing method is based upon torsion-oriented turbulization phenomena, which occur on the action of vibrational forces. Implementing the subject phenomenon allows the use of processing reactors without internal parts. This technological process is realized in a single-cavity hyperbolic chamber of the chemical reactor that is installed on the moving table of a vibration machine. The reactor's chamber is sealed with bottom and upper covers. The reactor and mobile table, forming the uniform vibrator—reactor system. The design of the reactor's housing provides a rigidity capable of resisting considerable external mechanical forces. This rigidity influences the deformation of the reactor's chamber's elements that continue to remain in the elastic tension zone.

Before discussing the subject phenomena, the concept of oscillation needs to be considered. In physics, oscillations are the processes that repeat exactly or approximately at regular intervals. Oscillations can occur when there are changes in fields of mechanical or electromagnetic forces. A different type of oscillation occurs when the stability of the internal state of systems in equilibrium changes because of the influence of external disturbing forces, changes in the heat balance or the volume of systems, and the tension in fields of internal pressure. Fields of internal pressure arise because of the pressure difference between adjacent volumes of the system. Such conditions are usually called natural or own oscillation. This kind of oscillation, as a rule, ceases to operate when the balance is restored.

Natural or own oscillations are the common form of the existence of a matter and are the basis of the Theory of Oscillations. They are the most important type of oscillations, given the conditions for the occurrence and the nature of all other types of oscillations that may arise in the system and depend on the nature of the own oscillations of the solutions or dispersion systems. When the frequency of the disturbing external vibrational forces approaches the frequency of the natural oscillation, the amplitude of the components of the dispersion system to be formed can sharply increase, causing the occurrence of the phenomenon called mechanical resonance.

To form a dispersion system, the components of it are loaded into the reactor's chamber. Both the reactor and the mixture of components inside the chamber are exposed to low-frequency vertically directed reciprocating sinusoidal disturbing forces with frequencies in the 30- to 150-Hz range, amplitudes in the 1- to 4-mm range and acceleration in the 20- to 50- G (gravity acceleration) range.

This resonance causes an essential increase in the amplitude of components processing dispersion systems. Thus, the mass of those systems comes up at high speed and strike the bottom surface of the top cover of the reactor, causing a rapid change of speed for the subject dispersion mass. In this case, the conditions for the occurrence of resonance require special consideration of the rheological and physicochemical characteristics of the dispersion system. Thus, it is fair to use the theory of the impact of a liquid on a rigid surface, when the impulses acting on a liquid and a rigid surface are determined. Knowledge of those impulses is necessary for calculating the rigidity and strength of the reactor's housing and reactor's covers [2-5].

Mathematically, the problem of the impact of an incompressible dispersed mass with a density ρ_0 on a rigid surface is reduced to finding the velocity potential:

$$v = \frac{p_i}{p_0},$$

where p_0 and p_i are an impulsive pressure and v is the harmonic function subject to the boundary conditions.

On the liquid's free surface $p = 0$, and on the contact surface of the dispersed liquid droplets, gas bubbles or solid particles with the inner surface of the upper cover of the reactor $\frac{\partial p}{\partial n} = a_n$, where a_n is the projection of the velocity of a given point on the surface of the dispersion system onto the normal one. In the considered particular case of the vertical impact of the dispersion system on the bottom surface of the reactor's upper cover, the system receives a vertical velocity a_y, in a direction opposite to the movement of the dispersion mass. The amount of the motion of the dispersed mass I_y and its kinetic energy K are determined by the expressions below:

$$I_y = m_y a_y;$$

$$K = \frac{m_y a_y^2}{2} = \frac{I_y a_y}{2},$$

where m is the generalized mass of the components of the emerging dispersion system.

As a result of the impact of the dispersion mass on the rigid surface of the upper cover, a shock wave is formed. It propagates through the dispersion mass in the opposite direction of the movement of the subject mass with supersonic speed. This shock wave represents a thin transition layer inside a dispersion system in which there is a sharp increase in the density, pressure and velocity of the substance.

The thickness of the transition layer is equal to the length of a free path of molecules. In the subject under question, shock waves are of interest only in which the direction of the velocity of the substance is perpendicular to the surface of the wave's front. When shock waves are passing through gas—air bubbles and a liquid medium, the parameters of these substances change in a discontinuous manner.

The values of the physical and physicochemical characteristics of dispersion systems on both sides of the shock wave are in ratio to one another arising because of the laws of mass conservation, momentum and energy. It should also be noted that the transition of shock waves changes the entropy of the substance. In this case, the jump in entropy is determined only by the law of conservation, which admits the existence of two modes: a jump in compression and a jump in relief of tension. However, in accordance with the second law of thermodynamics, the modes exist only when entropy increase.

As the shock wave propagates through the unperturbed mass, with the supersonic speed D is equal to

$$D = |\alpha_0| > \alpha_0.$$

The supersonic speed increases when the value of the intensity of the shock wave is greater and when the difference of pressure is greater on both sides of the shock wave. It also does so when an area of increased pressure is formed in front of the rapidly moving shock wave, while an area of reduced pressure is formed behind the wave. Thus, the shock wave is mechanically stable because any disturbances cannot penetrate the unperturbed medium, get ahead of the shock wave, or blur its front. With respect to the compressed matter located behind the front, the shock wave propagates at a subsonic speed that causes the thermodynamic regime behind the front of the shock wave to affects its amplitude. With an unlimited increase in the amplitude, the compression behind the front remains limited.

All of the above applies to the very first shock wave that reaches the reactor's bottom cover, is reflected by it, and begins to move in the opposite direction. Because the external disturbing forces act on the reactor with a certain frequency, the first shock wave is followed by the second, which is superimposed on the reflected first shock wave. The second wave is followed by the third wave, and so on.

These waves arise, move from the reactor's upper cover, and reach the reactor's bottom cover, which reflects them. These waves move through an already disturbed medium, that is, through zones of compression and depression. Shock waves meet and are superimposed upon one another, which causes the resonance cavitation phenomenon.

Considering the size of the bubbles and the thickness of the films of the dispersion medium surrounding the elementary volumes of solid particles, it is easy to assume that the forces acting on the surface of the bubbles are capillary—surface forces.

In this state the dispersion system is unstable. The number of forming bubbles grows rapidly. They group together, forming a zone in the central part of the reactor's chamber in which bubbles are most active. They vertically and horizontally oscillate, rotate, and collapse. The shock waves generated during their ruptures create a reduction in pressure inside the reactor, which contributes to the emergence of countless new bubbles.

In general, regardless of any origin, the cavitation phenomenon represents a disparaging process caused by continuity violation of the liquid environment and its transformation into a liquid–gas two–phase system or solid particles–bubbles–liquid three-phase system, whereas pressure in the liquid becomes equivalent to the pressure of saturated vapor of this liquid. At the same time, from a hydrodynamics perspective, any cavitation represents the process vapor—gas bubble formation in a volume of liquid resulting from the powerful influence of the external field of mechanical forces. In a broad sense of physicochemical dynamics, cavitation is the process of bubbles emerging in the exasperated liquid. Otherwise, it is a process of violations in a continuity of liquid that occurs without change in the ambient temperature.

Cavitation is indicated by a noise caused by the collapse of bubbles and is defined by the Cavitation Number K [8]:

$$K = \frac{2(\mathcal{P} - \mathcal{P}_V)}{\rho V^2},$$

(A)

or

$$\mathcal{P} = \frac{\kappa \rho V^2}{2} - \mathcal{P}_V,$$

(B)

where K is the cavitation number; $\mathcal{P}$ is the pressure inside the liquid, [H/m²]; $\mathcal{P}_V$ is the pressure of the steam, which is saturated by the liquid, [H/m²]; ρ is the liquid's density, [kg/m³]; and V is the speed of liquid flow, [m/s²].

The meaning of equation (A) is that cavitation bubbles begin to form when the pressure in the liquid, $\mathcal{P}$ falls below a critical value: $\mathcal{P}_{Cr}$ ($\mathcal{P} < \mathcal{P}_{Cr}$). In a liquid, the critical pressure, $\mathcal{P}_{Cr}$ is determined by the saturated vapor pressure inside the liquid at a certain ambient temperature and atmospheric pressure above the free surface of the liquid.

Because a certain amount of dissolved gas is constantly present in the liquid, under the condition ($\mathcal{P} < \mathcal{P}_{Cr}$), microscopic caverns are formed in the liquid volume. Those caverns are filled with the vapor of the dissolved gas and by the evaporation of the liquid itself, which penetrates as a result of diffusion. If the pressure inside the liquid falls below a certain value corresponding to the liquid's boiling point, intense evaporation of the liquid into the bubbles occurs through the interface. If the pressure inside the liquid remains below what the pressure is during boiling, gas prevails inside the bubbles.

As a result of the movement of the bubbles in the fluid flow, the growth of the bubbles that have fallen into the high pressure zone is limited and, under certain conditions, the bubbles are compressed to the dimensions corresponding to the surface pressure in the films surrounding them. Moving from one zone to another, these bubbles can change in size several times. However, in the areas of reduced pressure, the vapor—gas bubbles change their size with great speed and, as a result, collapse. This causes fluid hammer impact. This phenomenon is accompanied by a relatively loud sound impulse. The resulting shock wave propagates through the surrounding liquid. Moreover, the stronger the fluid hammer impact, the less vapor there is in the volume of the bubble.

Several known mechanisms can lead to the emergence of cavitation bubbles. The first type of cavitation consists of development in the flow of the liquid that is moving in the pipeline under the influence of an external source of a force field. Any flow restrictions cause differences in internal pressure in the adjacent zones, between which tensions are formed. This is likely explained by the deficiency of the liquid that results from the movement through the pipes of various sections. The quantity of liquid is simply not enough to maintain a continuous stream of liquid through the entire internal volume of a pipe.

The second type of cavitation consists of the formation of bubbles in the flow of the liquid moving under the influence of an external force field (for example, a ship screw or a pump impeller). As a result, differences in internal pressure form between adjacent zones of liquid, thus creating tension between these zones. However, these phenomena differ in that variations in pressure arise at the expense of the varying speeds of a stream's elementary volumes.

The third type of cavitation occurs under the influence of heat. When heating the tank containing the liquid, conditions are created on the hot surfaces of the device in the areas adjacent to the heat sources. Under these conditions, some volumes of liquid transition to a vaporous state. Other reasons for this type of cavitation are the effects of ultrasound, high-frequency electric discharge and flow around a surface with a high-speed gas stream (e.g., the surface of the fuselage or the wing of an airplane).

One shared fact among the above types of cavitation is that this phenomenon arises only in local volumes of liquid, adjacent to the external borders of liquid or gas. The consideration of all occurrences and mechanisms of the abovementioned types of cavitation nor detailed research on their nature are far beyond the scope of this work.

TORSION-ORIENTED PHENOMENON

Until recently, physics considered four states of matter: solid, liquid, gaseous and plasma, including fields of various natures and elementary particles. Recently, theoretical physics has been mastering the fifth level of reality: the physical vacuum. A. Akimov [9] and G. Shipov [10] proposed the opinion that the main state of any kind of matter, and the source of all particles and fields without exception, is a physical vacuum: that is, what remains in space when all gas and every last elementary particle is removed from it.

The concept of torsion fields was first used by the French mathematician Elie Cartan in 1913. He was the first person to say quite definitely, there must be fields based on rotation in nature.

The first scientist who developed a method for studying torsion fields was N.Karpov. The literature includes references to the works of the experimenters V. Kasyanov and F. Okhatrin who obtained photographs of the subject fields. Great contributions to the study of torsion fields were made by E. Fradkin, D. Gitman, V.Bagrov, D. Ivanenko, and I. Buchbinder, as well as other scientists [11-19]. Data also exist from research in this area carried out by scientific groups led by physicists D. Radin [20], A. Jafari [21], N. Nausaka [22], S. Imoushi [23], D. Sabbata [24, 25] and others. The discovery of new possibilities in physics and the development of vacuum physics bring changes to a wide variety of areas of knowledge: mechanics, quantum mechanics, astrophysics, physics of fields and elementary particles.

Recently, a whole range of torsion technologies has been developed. These technologies cover all sectors of the economy. The area of torsion technologies comprises torsion energy, torsion transport, communications, structural materials, geology and geophysics, chemical production, ecology, disposal of nuclear waste and cleaning of territories from radioactive contamination, agriculture and medicine.

After the researchers discovered that torsion fields could change the structure of crystals. Change of metals' crystal structure were obtained when the dynamic radiation of a torsion generator was applied to melts of some metals in a Tamman furnace. To conduct those experiments the furnace was designed as a vertical cylindrical. Its crucible was made of refractory steel. Above and below the cylinder, it is closed with covers. The metal under study was placed in the crucible inside the Tamman furnace. After the metal had melted, a torsion generator located outside the crucible was turned on. For 30 minutes, the torsion generator irradiated the metal melting. During this time, it was cooled from 1,400 °C to 800 °C. Then it was cooled and cut, and a physicochemical analysis was performed, the results of which showed that the crystal lattice pitch of the metal irradiated by the torsion field changed throughout the ingot volume, and in some cases the metal even acquired an amorphous structure.

Changes in torsion fields is accompanied by a change in the characteristics of dispersion systems and is accompanied by the release of energy. A torsion field is formed around a rotating object and is a set of micro-vortices of space. Because matter consists of atoms and molecules, and atoms and molecules have their own moment of rotation, matter always has a torsion field. A rotating dispersed system also has a torsion field. Torsion fields can arise due to the special geometry of space. Torsion charges of the same sign (direction of rotation) are attracted (i.e., like attracts like). The main properties of torsion fields are as follows:

- Torsion fields can interact, exchange information, and combine.
- Large torsion vortices can absorb small ones, and small ones can merge and form one large one.
- Streams swirling in one direction attract one another; differently swirling streams are repelled one another.
- One large vortex creates many small ones around itself that are opposite in direction.

THERMODYNAMICS OF DISPERSION SYSTEMS

The condition of the dispersion systems is characterized by an excess of free energy. Moreover, the integration of particles of the dispersed phase happens spontaneously, causing the reduction of free energy U. Thus, dispersion systems are unstable in a thermodynamic sense. Their temporary stability depends on the existence of the power barrier to prevent rapprochement and the fixing of elementary volumes and particles at rather small distances from each other (aggregation), the full association of droplets in emulsions and fogs, or the association of bubbles of gas in foams (coalescence). In a dispersed state, although steady for coalescence, separate solid particles are united in somewhat large units and form a so–called coagulative structure. They keep their identity as a result of layers of the dispersion liquid. The destruction of the films of surface separation causes the full associations of elementary volumes of the liquid phase in foams and emulsions or the emergence of direct contacts between microscopically small solid objects in suspensions or colloidal solutions.

The influence of modes on the formation of different kinds of dispersion systems and on their stability is especially important. The primary feature of the systems in question is the existence of a highly determined surface of separation among elements of the dispersed phase and the dispersion phase with the coefficient of surface tension σ. The main contribution to the change of free energy caused by the minimization of substances of system components comes from atoms located on the surface among phases. The number of atoms is comparable to their number in the volume of the substance that forms the dispersion environment.

As we considered earlier [5], the physical characteristic of a turbulent state is the potential difference of the internal pressure developing between the elementary volumes of the dispersion medium. At the same time, the considered turbulent state of a moving dispersed system is characterized by the indefinite compressibility of the liquid phase, the presence of numerous, constantly changing, and indefinite discontinuities in the continuity of the dispersion medium, and an indefinite motion of particles of a solid and a gas-liquid mixture, which have six degrees of freedom. Obviously, such a movement cannot be described by analytical methods. The only way to describe the nature of the motion of such a system in the first approximation is by vector analysis.

Before continuing the mathematical and physicochemical analysis of the initial stage of vibration impact on the reactor, it is necessary to consider the question: *is it* possible to consider a dispersion system as a thermodynamic system?

A thermodynamic system is any macroscopic system (in any state—solid, liquid or gas, or a multicomponent mix) that is in equilibrium from a thermodynamics position, or close to it [26,27]. However, such a definition does not exclude the possibility of a system condition in which one or several of its parameters within elementary volumes or points of this system differ from one another. For instance, we could assume the existence of systems in which temperature changes from one point of measurement to another and systems (gas, liquid, or system gas–liquid) in which the internal pressure in various elementary volumes differs from one another. It is obvious that, in these systems, the phenomena of heat exchange and a mass transfer would be observed. Such conditions do not remain invariable over time if they are not supported by an additional inflow of energy. Otherwise, after some time, a state is established in which the parameter values at all points or elementary volumes of the system remain unchanged for an arbitrarily long time if external conditions do not change and there is no influx of additional energy. Such states are considered to be in equilibrium.

The thermodynamic system transition process from a state of nonequilibrium to one of equilibrium is called a relaxation. For averaging or otherwise, when aligning values of each parameter in all volumes of a system, there is a characteristic time that is called a relaxation time for this parameter. The total relaxation time falls on the longest of all relaxation times. Estimations of the relaxation time for various processes cannot be made within the framework of thermodynamics. Physical kinetics deals with this issue.

Now, let us consider that a process in a thermodynamic system proceeds with a speed significantly lower than the speed of relaxation. This means that, at any point in such a process, all parameters would begin to level out. Such a process represents a chain of equilibrium states indefinitely close to one another. These rather slow processes can be called equilibrium or quasi-static processes. It should be noted that during equilibrium processes, the gradients of all parameters are equal to zero at any moment. It follows that because of symmetry, the process in the system can go in both directions—any system parameters can increase or decrease. Therefore, in the direct process, alignment can be reversed in time. In this regard, equilibrium processes can be considered reversible.

Thus, at the initial stage of the formation of dispersion systems in the mode of resonance cavitation, the system quickly goes into equilibrium upon the termination of the disturbing force. It is possible to apply standard thermodynamic methods to analyze these systems.

At the next stage of the formation of dispersion systems upon transition from resonance cavitation into the torsion-oriented turbulization mode, opposing hydraulic hammer shocks and, consequently, multidirectional shock waves arise. This situation is complicated by the fact that hydraulic hammer shock impacts and shock waves are physically different in nature. Hydraulic shock impacts arise upon the impact of the mixture components on the top cover of the reactor, whereas shock waves result from the collapse of the vapor–gas bubbles. This mass formation, development and rupture of vapor-gas bubbles could become relatively irreversible.

Under such conditions, in the presence of chaotic shock waves, it is not possible to talk of the temperature of the mixture at a certain point (to consider this process as isothermal), nor it possible to talk about a low rate of temperature change, constant pressure, or the reversibility of an isothermal process. Under these conditions, the concepts of entropy or enthalpy, as well as thermodynamic potentials, need additional definitions—if this is even possible in principle.

Consequently, upon transition to the resonance turbulization regime, characterized by the simultaneous and combined mechanical resonance action and fluid hammer phenomena, the process of forming dispersion systems becomes irreversible. In this case, they cannot be analyzed using regular thermodynamic methods. At the same time, all dispersion systems, regardless of how they are formed, are separated over time into constituent initial components after the termination of the action of an external perturbing force—relaxation. Therefore, for a final solution to this issue, additional research is required.

TORSION—ORIENTED TECHNOLOGICAL PROCESSES

At present, in astronomy, mechanics, and physics, a lot of observations have been accumulated related to the spontaneous ordering of the mutual arrangement of rotating subjects. These and many other experiments indicate the dependence of the energy of the system on its total rotation. Because in these experiments only the direction of the rotations changed but not their magnitude, it is necessary to consider not only torsion interactions, which consist in the transfer of the angular momentum of rotation, but also processes that can be called torsion-oriented processes.

According to Dr. V. Etkin, who contribution greatly to theoretical studies of torsion-oriented processes [28, 29], interest in them has increased in connection with the search for the so-called "fifth force", that is, the total interaction of force fields that differ from gravitational and electromagnetic ones. Meanwhile, a huge number of facts underlying the thermodynamics of irreversible processes [30] indicate that any real process arises under the action of all forces acting in the system (Onsager's theorem) so that its character and direction are determined by the ratio of these forces and their degree of involvement in a particular process.

Onsager's theorem [31], is one of the main theorems of thermodynamic irreversible processes, establishes the symmetry property of the kinetic coefficients for cross phenomena. In thermodynamic systems (in which there are gradients of temperature), concentrations of components and chemical potentials, irreversible processes of mass transfer, heat exchange, and chemical reactions arise. These processes are characterized by mass and heat potential, rates of chemical reactions, etc. They are given by the general term flows, and their causes (the deviations of thermodynamic parameters from equilibrium values) are called thermodynamic forces.

This is especially true for the processes occurring at the junction of the phenomena when the indicated forces have a different physical nature. Therefore, it would be correct to speak about a specific process that arises under the action of already known forces that lead to the order of the orientation of rotating systems or their parts, instead of an unknown force generated by an unknown interaction of various kinds of forces.

If a specific process of forming a dispersion system is associated with the transfer of the rotational acceleration of this system to elements of the dispersed phase, Dr. V. Etkin proposed to call them torsion-oriented processes [32]. Consideration of these processes, in his opinion, is advisable from the standpoint of thermo-kinetics, a unified theory of the mass transfer and of internal energy [33], as well as from the standpoint of energy dynamics and their further influence on the processes of conversion of various forms of energy [34].

LAW OF ENERGY CONSERVATION FOR DISPERSION SYSTEMS

It is known that classical thermodynamics expresses changes in the internal energy of the system U as a reversible (quasi-static) process. In general, the product of the total (generalized) potential Ψ_i (temperature T, pressure P, chemical potential of the k-th substance M_k, so on) by the change in the generalized coordinate of the physical parameters θ_i (entropy $\mathbb{S}$, volume — V (with the minus sign), the mass of the k-th substance $M_{k,}$ and so on) [30, 31]:

$$dU = Td\mathbb{S} - PdV + \sum_k \mu_k dM_k = \sum_i \Psi_i d\theta_{i,} \qquad (1)$$

where n_i ($i=1,2, ..., n$) is the number of degrees of freedom of the equilibrium system; TdS is the elementary heat exchange of the system; dQ; PdV is the elementary work of expansion; and $\mu_k dM_k$ is the energy exchange of the k-th substance across the boundaries of the equilibrium system dU_k.

For equilibrium systems expressed in general form by equation (1), the change in the generalized coordinate is due to the transfer of a certain amount of it across the boundaries of the system. This allows expressing the change in the parameters θ_i over time t to be expressed as

$$\frac{d\theta_i}{dt} = -\int j_i n df, \qquad (2)$$

where $j = \rho_i w_i$ is the flux density of the physical parameter θ_i through the closed surface of the system f in the direction of the outer normal n; $\rho_i = \frac{d\theta_i}{dV}$ is the density of the parameters θ_i; $w_i = v_i - v_m$ is the speed of movement of its element $d\theta_i = \rho_i dV$ with respect to the center of mass of the elementary volume dV; and $v_i = \frac{\overrightarrow{dr_i}}{dt}$ and $v_m = \frac{\overrightarrow{dr_m}}{dt}$, $\overrightarrow{r_i}$, and $\overrightarrow{r_m}$ are the radius vectors (respectively) of the element of the i-th physical parameter $d\theta_i$ and an element of mass dM in a fixed system of coordinate.

Substituting equation (2) into equation (1), is the following:

$$\frac{dU}{dt} = -\sum_i \Psi_i \int j_i n df \qquad (3)$$

Equation (3) is a consequence of a general expression:

$$\frac{dU}{dt} = -\sum_i \int \psi_{ij} j_i n df \qquad (4)$$

For a particular case of a homogeneous system, when the local value of the function ψ_i of the generalized potential, then Ψ_i is equal at all points of the system and therefore can be taken outside the integral sign, where ψj_i is the i-th component of the internal energy density $j_u = \sum_i \psi_i j_i$ through the element df of the surface of the system located relative to the fixed system of coordinates.

Based on the Ostrogradsky–Gauss theorem [35], the equation (3) could be reduced to an integral over the volume of the system. The expression for the energy conservation law for an arbitrary region of the continuum can be written in the following form:

$$\frac{dU}{dt} = -\int div j_u \, dV. \qquad (5)$$

Now, if

$$divj_u = \sum_i \, div(\psi_i j_i),$$

that the expanded form of equation (5) could be presented as the sum of two terms:

$$\sum_i \psi_i \, divj_i + \sum_i j_i grad\psi_i.$$

Or

$$\frac{dU}{dt} = - \sum_i \psi_i \, div \, j_i + \sum_i i \, X_i j_i, \qquad (6)$$

where $X_i = - grad\psi_i$ is the driving force of the i-th process, called in the theory of irreversible processes thermodynamic force in its energy representation.

In comparison with equation (1), the equation (6) contains a doubled number of terms, if additional members are related to processes that are not characteristic of homogeneous systems. First of all, these are processes of energy dissipation, leading to a spontaneous change in a number of thermodynamic parameters (entropy S, volume V, mass of the k-th substance M_k, etc.) due to viscosity, expansion into cavities, chemical reactions, etc.

The balance equation of these quantities

$$\frac{d\rho_i}{dt} = - \, div \, j_i + \sigma_i, \qquad (7)$$

is considered by introducing the density of internal sources of this quantity σ_i [30].

The div j_i reflects the change in the quantity ρ_i because of the transfer of the physical parameters θ_i across the boundaries of the system, which takes place during mass transfer, heat exchange, volumetric deformation, etc. Also, by considering the equation (7), equation (6) takes the following form:

$$\frac{dU}{dt} = \Sigma_i \int \psi_i (d\rho_i/dt)dV + \Sigma_i \int \psi_i \sigma_i \, dV +$$
$$+ \Sigma_i \int X_i j_i \, dV. \tag{8}$$

It is easy to see that in systems in equilibrium (externally and internally) in which the thermodynamic force $X_i = 0$ and the function of the generalized potential $\psi_i = \Psi_i$, there are no internal sources σ_i, and this equation transforms into equation (1). Consequently, the terms of the third sum (8) can refer only to the work W_i by the system being performed in addition to the work of the extension.

For the sake of simplification, let us consider the thermodynamic force X_i and the speed of displacement v_i constant over the volume of the system. Therefore, taking them outside the integral sign, we have the following:

$$\int X_i j_i \, dV = \int X_i v_i \, d\theta_i = F_i v_i, \tag{9}$$

where $F_i = \theta_i X_i$.

This expression (9) corresponds to the definition of the work (power) of the i-th process $N_i = \frac{dW_i}{dt}$ as the excretion of the resulting force F_i by the speed v_i of the object of application of this value v_i. As a result, the thermodynamic force X_i becomes simple and understandable in the Newtonian understanding of the force referred to the i-th physical quantity $(X_i = \frac{F_i}{\theta_i})$.

According to equation (8), in the process of doing work, energy can pass from one (for example, i-th) form to any other form (for example, j-th), including thermal (thus, the energy can dissipate). This circumstance makes equation (6) valid for processes with any degree of dissipativity, and it allows one to obtain from equation (8) the expression that is fundamental in the theory of irreversible processes for the rate of entropy occurrence in stationary processes

$$\left(\frac{dU}{dt} = 0\right)$$

[33].

Thus, the proposed form of the law of the conservation of energy differs from the form of the law used in the mechanics of a continuous medium and the thermodynamics of irreversible processes [30]. This brings into consideration an additional processes of energy conversion, accompanied by the performance of useful work W_i including energy dissipation.

In cases when the system performs a rotational motion, then an additional term is added to the right side of equation (1):

$$\sum \mathfrak{G}_\alpha \, d\theta_{\omega\alpha} ,$$

where $\mathfrak{G}_\alpha$ and $\theta_{\omega\alpha}$ are the components of the angular velocity vector $\vec{\mathfrak{G}}_\alpha$ (at $\alpha = 1,2,3$) and the angular momentum $\theta_\omega = I\mathfrak{G}$, and I is the moment of inertia of the body.

Thus, the term appears in the second sum of equation (6) $X_{\omega\alpha} j_{\omega\alpha}$, where $X_{\omega\alpha} = - \vec{\mathbb{N}}\omega_\alpha$, $j_{\omega\alpha} = \rho_\omega w_\omega$ are components of the vector-gradient of the angular velocity $\vec{\mathbb{N}}\mathfrak{G}$ and the tensor of the flux density of the angular momentum, where $\rho_\omega = \vec{I}\theta_\omega / \vec{I}V$, and w_ω is the relative velocity of moment transfer amount of motion. These terms characterize the processes of transfer of the rotational momentum in systems with an inhomogeneous field of angular velocity of rotation.

It was suggested in works[9, 10] to call this kind of interaction torsional. It should be noted that, according to equation (6), the transfer of vorticity [32]—in particular, the turbulent transfer of momentum—is possible in media with a moment of inertia, when $I \neq 0$.

Considering processes occurring in homogeneous systems, it can be carried out, as the radius vector $\vec{r_i}$ of the element $d\theta_i$ is expressed by the vector $\vec{e_i}$, which is characterized by the modulus $|r_i|$ of this vector. Therefore, in the general case, its change is expressed by two terms:

$$d\vec{r_i} = d_\varphi \vec{r_i} + d_r \vec{r_i} = e_i d\vec{r_i} + \vec{r_i} de_i. \qquad (9)$$

In equation (9), the left-hand side $d_\varphi \vec{r_i}$ characterizes the transfer of the element $d\theta_i$ without changing the transfer direction e_i, and the second term $d_r \vec{r_i}$ characterizes the change in the direction of this vector.

It is more convenient to express the value of de_i through the vector of the rotation angle φ, normal to the plane of rotation formed by the vectors $\vec{e_i}$ and the increment of this vector $d\vec{e_i}$ In this case, the increment de_i is determined by the product of vectors $d\vec{\varphi_i}$ and $\vec{e_i}$, that

$$r_i de_i = [d\varphi_i, r_i]$$

and

$$X_i \times [d\varphi_i, r_i] = d\varphi_i \times [r_i, X_i].$$

Considering equations (7) and (8), the equation (6) could be presented as follows:

$$\frac{dU}{dt} - \sum_i \int \psi_i (d\rho_i / dt) dV + \sum_i \int \psi_i \sigma_i \, dV +$$
$$+ \sum_i \int X_i \cdot j_i^c \, dV + \sum_i \int M_i (d\varphi_i / dt) \rho_i dV \qquad (10)$$

where $j_i^c = r_i e_i \dfrac{dr_i}{dt}$ is the displacement of the flux density of the element $d\theta_i$ relative to the center of mass of the system; $M_i = r_i X_i$ is the moment of force X_i; and $\dfrac{d\varphi_i}{dt}$ is the angular velocity of rotation of the element $d\theta_i$ relative to the center of mass of the system.

Equation (10), according to Dr. V. Etkin [32], is the most general and at the same time the most detailed of the known mathematical formulations of the energy conservation law. In addition to the processes of energy dissipation, mass transfer and heat exchange in the considered theory of irreversible processes and physical kinetics, the equation (10) describes the processes of reorientation of displacement vectors $d\vec{r_i}$, arising in the presence of moments M_i of thermodynamic forces X_i. Moreover, it contains two types of members responsible for rotation.

First, these are the terms of the third sum (10) containing the rotation forces $X_{\omega\alpha}$, which are rotational components of the vector-gradient of the angular velocity $\vec{N}\mathbb{G}$. These terms characterize the processes of transfer of the angular moments of motion, caused by the inhomogeneous distribution of the density of the angular moment of rotation of the subject (as well as their angular velocity ω).

The terms of the fourth sum of equation (10), containing the moments of forces M_i, determine the work done by the moment of force M_i per unit of time when the element $d\theta$ is reoriented at a speed of $X_e j_e$. However, in accordance with equations (9) and (10), these moments disappear when the direction of the vectors $\overrightarrow{X_i}$ and $d\overrightarrow{r_i}$ coincides. Therefore, according to Etkin [32], these moments of force should be called not rotation moments of forces but orientated moments of forces.

Unlike torsional phenomena, the orientation processes do not change the angular momentum of the system and its kinetic energy of rotation, affecting only the orientation of dispersed particles relative to external elements or fields (φ_i) (i.e., to a part of their potential energy $U(\varphi_i)$), which depends on their mutual orientation. In accordance with the thermodynamic principles of the classification of processes (distinguishing processes not for their causes them, and not for the physical nature of the interaction, but for their consequences), such processes should be called oriented.

NATURE OF ORIENTATION'S MOMENTS

A feature of the formation of dispersed systems (as a special case, inhomogeneous systems) under conditions of the joint and simultaneous action of mechanical resonance and the impact of numerous shock waves arising from exploding vapor–gas bubbles is the shift of the center of the extensive parameters θ_i. Those parameters are relative to the center of mass of the total dispersion system. This, to a certain extent, coincides with what was shown in Etkin's work [34].

It is known that the position of this center, the radius vector of which is designated $\overrightarrow{R_1}$ and is equal to the following:

$$\overrightarrow{R_1} = \frac{1}{\theta_i} \int \overrightarrow{r_i} \, d\theta_i$$

(11)

Let us suppose that the position of the center of the parameters θ_i in the homogeneous (equilibrium) system R_{io} is taken as the origin of the current coordinate r_i. In this case, $\Delta R_i = R_i - R_{io}$. So for any equilibrium state where the external R_m and the internal position R_{io} coincide, ΔR_i will determine the displacement of the center of parameters θ_i from the center of mass of the system R_m. Thus, under the action of the forces X_i in a dispersion system, a certain moment of distribution $\mathbf{Z}_i = \theta_i \Delta R_i$ of the parameter θ_i looks like this:

$$Z_i = \theta_i \Delta R_i = \int \overrightarrow{r_i} d\theta_i \, .$$

(12)

The redistribution of the parameters $\int \overrightarrow{r_i} d\theta_i$ can cause that some of the forces acting in the system with respect to the mass of the system to act off-center. Those forces, after being brought to the center of mass of the system, are forming oriented moments that tend to reorient the increment of the center of mass position ΔR_i in such a way that the forces $\mathbf{X}_i$ tend to act in-center.

A less obvious reason may be the presence of several oppositely directed forces X_i in the emerging dispersion system. According to the basic proposition of the theory of irreversible processes, each of the flows j_i arises under the total action of all forces of the same tensor rank X_j in the system (for $j = 1,2, ... n$). This assumption is in full compliance with Onsager's principle [31]:

$$j_i = \Sigma_i L_{ij} X_j, \qquad (13)$$

where L_{ij} are so-called phenomenological coefficients characterizing the conductivity of the system. Particular cases of equation (13) are the well-known laws of heat exchange (Fourier's), electrical conductivity (Ohm's), mass transfer (Fick's), filtration (Darcy's), viscosity (Newton's), and so on.

Thus, in accordance with modern concepts, forces of different natures generating one or another independent process are generally equal to the number of nonequilibrium degrees of freedom of the system. Thus, they cannot be reduced to the four known types of fundamental interactions. In this case, equations (13) reflects the interrelation of the processes resulting from the imposition of dissimilar forces X_j. This superposition leads to the emergence of numerous phenomena (thermomechanical, thermochemical, mechanochemical, etc.) [30, 31].

In particular, as it follows from equation (13), the process of the displacement of any parameter θ_i (for example, electric current) can arise not only from the forces of an electrical nature but also under the action of the thermomotion force $X_j = -\overrightarrow{N}T$. The last force along with the magnetic component of the Lorentz force, bends the trajectory of the electric charge and leads to the appearance of an electric field E in the direction of the force X_j. This phenomenon is called the thermomagnetic phenomenon [10].

Similarly, the process of the redistribution of electrical charges can also cause mechanical stresses X_{mech} (piezoelectric phenomenon). Thus, equations (6) and (10), instead of searching for a unified field theory, propose a unified method for finding the clearly distinguishable driving forces of various physicochemical processes, including the processes of heat transfer, mass transfer, transformation of rotational motion, and reorientation of inhomogeneities present in the system. These last processes arise under the action of the moments M_i tending to reorient the increments of the vectors $\overrightarrow{\Delta R_1}$ in the direction of their decrease. Since the vectors $\overrightarrow{M_1}$ and $\overrightarrow{d\varphi_1}$ were the result of the expansion of the second sum in equation (6) and reflect two sides of the same process of redistribution of the parameter θ_i, any equation similar to equation (12) could be written for the generalized rates of the reorientation process as follows:

$$\frac{\overrightarrow{d\varphi_1}}{dt} = \sum K_{ij}M_j \qquad (14)$$

where K_{ij} are phenomenological coefficients characterizing the compliance of dispersion systems to rotation.

As in equation (13), equation (14) reflects the fact that the process of the reorientation of the dispersion system can be caused by any of the moments M_j. In particular, this means that the process of orientation is influenced by various fields of forces: temperatures, differences in internal pressures between adjacent elementary volumes (the internal tension), and so on. Reorientation processes can also produce torsion fields characterized by the antisymmetric part of the tensor $\nabla \mathfrak{G}$.

During the experiments, the tornado-like formation of floating and simultaneously rotating vapor–gas bubbles was observed inside of the central part of the reactor. It is quite probable that this behavior of dispersed particles was caused by the action of some of the moments $\mathbf{M}_i$ on the rotating particles of the dispersed phase.

It is also known that the moment of force M_i, which must be applied to the axis of rotation to rotate it through an angle $d\varphi_i$ in time dt, is equal to the rate of change of the angular momentum θ_ω [36]

$$M_i = |\frac{d\varphi_i}{dt}| \times |\theta_\omega| \sin \varphi_i. \qquad (15)$$

Thus, it follows that for the same value of the disturbing moment M_i, the higher the angular moment θ_ω the smaller the angle φ_i. Therefore, when an additional angular moment θ_ω is imparted to the subject, the angle φ_i decreases (i.e. the orientation of the axes of rotation of the subjects becomes more organized). Thus, the change of the angular moment is also accompanied by a reorientation of the angular moment of the rotating components of the dispersed phase. These are the processes that V. Etkin called torsion-oriented [32]. This allows the considered process formation of dispersion systems to be considered as torsion-oriented turbulization.

From equation (10), any forms of ordered energy transfer and mass exchange can include components perceived by dispersion systems as their oriented polarization. This circumstance makes it superfluous to consider additional influences to explain the associated phenomena. According to the above, the existence of torsion and torsion-oriented interactions directly follows from the energy conservation law applicable to dispersion systems. Regardless of their nature, these interactions give rise to processes of orderly energy exchange, such as the ability to perform work.

Consideration of torsion-oriented turbulization and the corresponding interactions are of a purely thermodynamic nature. That statement does not claim to be a fully describe all details of the subject condition and therefore, it does not require the establishment of the nature of the mentioned interactions, or a structure of the system, or a mechanism of the energy it transfers. This approach makes it possible to draw a clear line between torsional and torsional-oriented phenomena. From the standpoint of energy dynamics, torsion interactions are generated by an inhomogeneous field of angular velocities of rotation of media possessing mass and a certain moment of inertia. In this case, the torsion-oriented impact is transmitted by known force fields.

The consideration of oriented processes is a definite step toward the study of the process of the dissolution of gases in the liquid and formation of dispersion systems. It provides a key to understanding the origin of such processes, finding their driving forces and clarifying their influence on the functional capabilities of nonequilibrium systems. When some relaxation processes occur in some parts or with degrees of freedom of a polyvariant system, their other parts or degrees of freedom can move away from equilibrium, which ensures the possibility of a long-term development of such systems, bypassing the state of equilibrium.

This is because the approach of the system to equilibrium is accompanied not only by energy dissipation but also by a useful transformation of energy. The internal work performed at the same time ensures the maintenance of a temporary order in the system, called dissipative structures. It is characteristic that in the most inhomogeneous system such useful transformations of energy can be caused not only by external force fields (e.g., electromagnetic and gravitational force fields) but also by the fields of temperatures, internal pressures (stresses), concentrations, etc.

This is of particular importance for understanding the causes of the emergence of the so-called processes of self-organization, which involves the performance of useful internal work of some parts of the system on others with the inevitable irreversibility (presence of losses) in both. In particular, equation (10) reveals the reasons for the emergence of the so-called dissipative structures, (i.e., ordered states maintained by dissipative processes in the system). In this case, the stationary state of partially ordered systems arises through the mutual compensation of two opposite processes - orientation (caused by performing work) and disorientation (caused by energy dissipation). It is especially important to understand that torsion-oriented turbulization can be spontaneous.

EFFICIENCY OF TORSION-ORIENTED TURBULIZATION

As considered earlier, dispersion systems possess several special characteristics including the excess of a free energy, super large surface separation between phases, elevated chemical activity, and others. Given the developed interface between phases, such systems are unstable. The main characteristic of dispersion system is the size of the specific surface, which is determined by the size of the surface related to the allocated volume of the dispersed phase carried to unit of the same volume. Also, the most important characteristic of the dispersion medium is its continuity.

The main research methods for mechanical phenomena are developed nonadditive, or otherwise, non-extensive thermodynamics. The concept of non-additivity (or otherwise, non-extensiveness) assumes that some thermodynamic, mechanical and physical properties of system do not depend on the change of volume in the system.

Additivity or non-additivity are defined by the relation between an integral object and its components. The concept of additivity can be expressed by the following definition: the whole is equal to the sum of its parts. For non-additivity can be presented as the whole is not equal to the sum of its parts. Furthermore, if the whole is less than the sum of its parts, then it defines sub-additivity. Conversely, if the whole is larger than the sum of its parts, this defines the concept of super-additivity.

To further develop these representations, it is possible to assume that any additive material system has additive properties. For example, the mass of the physical system is equal to the sum of the masses of the parts of this system. Because many properties of those complicated systems are not additive, they do not have similar properties to other parts of the system.

And also, if they do not interact definitely the non-additivity of the system assumes the difference between properties of this system and the sum of properties of elements of the same system.

In orthodox thermodynamics the major geometrical parameter is the volume. As a rule, volume and related thermodynamic functions are extensive and independent of a geometrical form of the system. Therefore, the dispersion systems, as a rule, differ in the non-extensiveness of the entropy, thermodynamic functions and other physical characteristics.

Considering the complicated heterogeneous systems as solid particles–liquid, solid particles–liquid–liquid, and liquid–gas, that are under the influence of the external revolting field of forces, it is possible to assume that any thermodynamic system possesses non-extensive properties.

The sign of the completion formation of dispersion systems under vibration in the mode of resonance cavitation and torsion-oriented turbulization is the rupture of a continuum of the dispersion medium.

Also, as noted earlier that the considered phenomenon of torsion-oriented turbulization arises under conditions in which the components of the future dispersion systems are placed in the chemical reactor. The necessary requirements for the reactor's chamber are a single cavity hyperbolic shape and rigidity. The chamber assumes the formation of dispersion systems under the influence of the external revolting force trying to change the volume of the formed system. The reactor's chamber rigidity resists a change in the internal volume of the reactor chamber. Thus, the process of the dissolving gases in liquid and the formation of dispersion systems occurs at a constant volume.

The phenomena of mechanical resonance and fluid (hydraulic) hammer impact, arising at certain parameters of vibration, lead to resonance cavitation and torsion-oriented turbulization, which is the condition of the dissolving gases in liquid and of the formation of dispersion systems.

As already repeatedly noted, the physical and chemical processes happening at the molecular level, including heat exchange and a mass transfer, are on the separation surface and through an interface between phases. For this reason, the main problem of modern chemical, thin technologies and nanotechnologies is the increase of the interface.

The main objective of research on the efficiency of chemical processes using traditional physicochemical technology methods is to define the certain parameters as a function of time, under controlled thermodynamic conditions.

SPEED OF DISOLUTION GASES AND FORMATION OF DISPERSION SYSTEMS

For research on the speed of the process of the solution gases in liquid and the formation of dispersion systems in the mode of torsion-oriented turbulization, it is necessary to add to the usual conditions parameters of vibration where the subject phenomenon occurs. Thus, the target of this research is to find the corresponding equation that will allow for modeling the considered technological process [5]. Usually, such equations could be determined by an experimental method.

For the purpose of determining the kinetic equation, the first of all, it is necessary to test the stoichiometric equation of the reaction. The stoichiometric equation is the chemical formula describing the ideal combined structure of a chemical compound from atoms, that meets the requirement of valency (i.e., the ability of the atom to form chemical bonds with other atoms or groups of atoms).

Let us consider a rather trivial situation where the speed of chemical reaction in the mode of torsion-oriented turbulization is the function of time and the parameters of vibration. Let us consider a virtual process:

$$aA + \text{в}B \rightarrow cC + ...,$$

It describes the formation of a dispersion system with the conditions of a constant volume of the reactor V and a constant temperature T. The kinetic equation of such a process has the following appearance:

$$\frac{dv}{dt} = k \, (n_{a0} - x)^a \, (n_{a0} - \frac{bx}{u})^b,$$ (16)

where a, b and k are permanent amounts of substances, that have to be defined for each process on the basis of the experimental data.

In equation (16), the internal space of the chemical reactor's chamber V is permanent and the total area of the phase's interface is included and composed of the same constant of chemical process k. In some cases, dispersion systems are formed parallel with collateral chemical reactions. As the result of which multicomponent and multiphase dispersion systems are formed with blurry phases and a weakly expressed dispersion medium.

It is necessary to understand, that at the point of the occurrence of the phenomenon of torsion-oriented turbulization, the total size of the phase interface is a function of the parameters of vibration, surface tension, and the geometrical dimensions of the internal chamber of the chemical reactor. It is quite obvious that, in the maintenance of the mode of resonance turbulization when the formed dispersion system is in a turbulent state, the size of the phase interface changes constantly.

For the determining the speed of the formation of the dispersion systems in the modes, such as torsion-oriented turbulization, it is useful to conduct the vector analysis of the general motion of the medium of the processing dispersion system.

Let us consider the movement of the dispersion medium within the dispersion system, which is formed under the influence of an external force field in the mode of torsion-oriented turbulization.

This formation of the dispersion system is followed by an emergence, development and a collapse of vapor–gas bubbles. The density of the dispersion environment ρ (x, y, z, t) changes over time. The vector of the speed of this environment's movement can be designated through vector $\overrightarrow{\mathfrak{W}}$.

In the flow of the dispersion phase, let us allocate the motionless elementary volume V, limited by a surface S. The liquid flows through an allocated surface on an elementary platform dS. As this occurs, the amount of the liquid and its mass are equal:

$$\rho \overrightarrow{\mathfrak{W}}_n dS. \qquad (17)$$

During the same period of time, the amount of the mass of this liquid Q flows through the total surface S:

$$Q = \iint_S \rho \overrightarrow{\mathfrak{W}}_n dS. \qquad (18)$$

Conversely, the mass of the iquid contained in volume V is equal:

$$\iiint_V \rho \, dV. \qquad (19)$$

During the considered unit of time the mass of the liquid will change to the following:

$$\iiint_V \frac{\partial \rho}{\partial t} \, dV. \qquad (20)$$

Therefore, during a some period of time an amount of liquid will flow from the considered volume that is equal to the following:

$$Q = -\iiint_V \frac{\partial \rho}{\partial t} \, dV. \qquad (21)$$

After the equilibrium of the right parts of equations (18) and (19), will be as follows:

$$\iint_S \rho\overrightarrow{\mathfrak{W}}_n \, dS = -\iiint_V \frac{\partial\rho}{\partial t} \, dV. \tag{22}$$

Applying Ostrogradsky's formula [35] to the integral standing in the left part of expression (22), will result in the following:

$$\iiint_V \left[\frac{\partial\rho}{\partial t} + \operatorname{div}(\rho\overrightarrow{\mathfrak{W}})\right] dV. \tag{23}$$

Because the volume V is taken randomly, the inner part of equation (23) equals as:

$$\frac{\partial\rho}{\partial t} + \nabla \cdot (\rho\overrightarrow{\mathfrak{W}}) = 0. \tag{24}$$

Equation (24) is the main equation of the fluid dynamics. Its physical meaning is the condition of the dispersion phase continuity.

For incompressible liquid the density ρ is constant. In this case, $\frac{\partial\rho}{\partial t} = 0$

$$\rho(\nabla \cdot \overrightarrow{\mathfrak{W}}) = 0. \tag{25}$$

If the flow of liquid moves forward without rotation, the following is the case:

$$\nabla \cdot \overrightarrow{\mathfrak{W}} = 0. \tag{26}$$

In this case, vector $\overrightarrow{\mathfrak{W}}$ is a gradient of a scalar function φ (x, y, z), and

$$\overrightarrow{\mathfrak{W}} = \nabla\varphi.$$

From the equation (25), for the incompressible liquid, equation (26) will be equal to 0.

Therefore, function φ must satisfy the next equation:

$$\nabla \nabla \varphi = 0, \qquad (27)$$

or

$$\text{div grad } \varphi = 0. \qquad (28)$$

Equation (28) is a so-called Laplace's Equation. It determines the speed potential for moving of the incompressible liquid.

In physics, the concept of speed is usually associated with the movement of a material point. In the case in question—the movement of a compressible dispersion system—the separate adjacent elementary volumes move at different speeds. Thus, instead of considering linear speed, it is more appropriate to consider the *gradient* of linear speed. For the gradient of linear speed for moving in a dispersion system in which various layers (zones, volumes) are moving at different speeds, it is acceptable to define the change of linear speed related to the unit of the distance between different layers (zones, volumes) as follows:

$$\text{grad } \overrightarrow{\mathfrak{W}} = \frac{dw}{dh}.$$

If there is a uniform change in speed in the unit of the thickness of the film of a dispersion system's cross section, the following is the case:

$$\text{grad } \overrightarrow{\mathfrak{W}} = \frac{1}{h}(w_2 - w_1),$$

where grad $\overrightarrow{\mathfrak{W}}$ is the gradient of linear speed; dW is the infinitely small change in speed; dh is the infinitely small distance between layers (films), which corresponds to changes in speed dw; and $(w_2 - w_1)$ is the change in speed in two layers of a dispersion system that are at distance h from each other.

Similarly, instead of linear acceleration, it would be correct to consider the acceleration gradient as the change of linear acceleration upon the distance between the layers (zones, volumes) of a dispersion system:

$$\text{grad } \mathcal{A} = \frac{dw}{dh},$$
$$\text{grad } \mathcal{A} = \frac{1}{h}(a_2 - a_1),$$

where grad $\mathcal{A}$ is the gradient of linear acceleration; $d\mathcal{A}$ is the infinitely small change in acceleration; dh is the infinitely small distance h between layers relating to changes in acceleration $d\mathcal{A}$; and $(a_2 - a_1)$ is the change in acceleration in two layers of a dispersion system that are at distance dh from each other.

SURFACE TENSION AND INTERFACE BETWEEN PHASES

In the classical understanding of the surface tension σ represents the thermodynamic characteristic of the interface between two phases that are in balance. This is determined by the work of isothermal A (at temperature T) and the reversible formation of the unit of the area S_{12} under the condition that the temperature, volume and chemical potentials of all components in both phases of the system are remain constant:

$$\sigma_{12} = \left(\frac{A}{S_{12}}\right) T.$$

The chemical potential represents the thermodynamic function, used to describe the condition of a system with a variable number of particles. It defines the change of thermodynamic potentials, such as enthalpies and internal energy. It also represents the energy of bringing one particle into the system without the commissioning of work.

Surface tension has different meanings in energy and power. Its energy (thermodynamic) definition in surface tension is the specific work of increasing a surface when it is stretched under conditions of constant temperature. Its power (mechanical) definition in surface tension is the force acting on a unit length of a line that limits the surface of a liquid.

The force of surface tension is directed on a tangent to the surface of the liquid, which is perpendicular to the site of a contour and is proportional to the length of the counter of this surface. The force acting on this counter per unit of the length is called "the coefficient of a surface tension" and is marked as σ. Upon a rupture of the unit of the surface [m^2], it is better to provide the definition of the surface tension as a unit of energy [J]. In this case, there is a clear physical sense of the concept of the surface tension.

Surface tension acts on the perimeter of separation between phases— liquids, gases, and solids. In the case in question, surface tension could be considered to be the force, acting per unit of the length of the counter of the surface and aspiring to reduce this surface to a minimum at the set volumes of phases.

The free surface of liquid is connected to the concept of free energy U :

$$U \, Sr = \sigma S,$$

where σ is the coefficient of the surface tension, [N/m = J/m^2]; and S is the full surface area of liquid [m^2].

As the free energy U of the isolated system aspires to a minimum, the liquid (for lack of external force fields) seeks to take the form with the smallest possible surface area. Thus, the task of forming the liquid comes down to the solution of the isoperimetric task of finding the three-dimensional geometric object that has the largest volume among all bodies with the same surface area. This object is, as we know, the sphere.

Let us consider the full free surface that arises when forming a dispersion system using resonance turbulization. In Euclidean geometry, the concept of a surface is accepted as a two-dimensional topological variety. In real life, in three–dimensional space, the concept of a surface is accepted as an external perimeter of a system. In mathematics the concept of a function assumes the existence of a point at which the mathematical object that is a mathematical function is disputable. That is, there is a point at which the function loses its continuity; in other words, the function becomes undifferentiated or singular.

Usually, a surface S can be presented as a number of material points with the coordinates satisfying the following:

$$S\ (xyz) = 0. \qquad (29)$$

If at some point of time function $S(xyz)$ is continuous and occurs in continuous private derivatives—at least one of which is not equal to zero—near this point the surface satisfying equation (27) is considered to be the correct.

The most important attribute of a surface S is an area that can be determined by the following:

$$S = \iint [r_u \times r_v]\ du\ dv. \qquad (30)$$

where $r_u = \{\dfrac{dx}{du}, \dfrac{dy}{du}, \dfrac{dz}{du}\}$ and $r_v = \{\dfrac{dx}{dv}, \dfrac{dy}{dv}, \dfrac{dz}{dv}\}$.

Transforming expression (30) for defining a surface, will be is as follows:

$$S = \iint \sqrt{(\tfrac{df}{dx})^2 + (\tfrac{df}{dy})^2 } + dxdy. \qquad (31)$$

The formula for defining a surface that is accepted as the solution for a parametrical task is the following:

$$S = \iint \sqrt{(\frac{D(x,y)}{D(u,v)})^2 + (\frac{D(y,z)}{D(u,v)})^2 + (\frac{D(z,x)}{D(u,v)})^2} \, dudv.$$ (32)

Substituting the value S from equation (32) in an expression for the free energy of $U_{Sr,}$ the general meaning of free energy in a dispersion system is the following:

$$U_{Sr} = \sigma \iint \sqrt{(\frac{D(x,y)}{D(u,v)})^2 + (\frac{D(y,z)}{D(u,v)})^2 + (\frac{D(z,x)}{D(u,v)})^2} \, dudv.$$ (33)

The free vapor–gas bubble takes a spherical form; however, under complicated conditions, the task of forming the surface of a bubble becomes extremely difficult.

Let us consider a thin liquid film whose thickness can be disregarded. Seeking to minimize the free energy, the film creates a difference in pressure on both of its sides. The film shrinks until the pressure inside the bubble does not exceed the atmospheric pressure at the amount of the additional pressure from this film. The additional pressure at the surface point depends on the average surface curvature at this point and is defined by using Laplace's formula:

$$\Delta P_S = \sigma k = \sigma \left(\frac{1}{r_1} + \frac{1}{r_2}\right).$$ (34)

where r_1 and r_2 are the radiuses of the main curvature at the point.

If the relevant centers of curvature lie on one side of the tangent plane in the considered point, then the radiuses have an identical sign. The opposite is also true: radiuses have the different signs, if they lie on the different sides of the tangent plane. For example, in

DR. LEV G. AMUSIN, PH.D.

a sphere, the centers of curvature at any point coincide with the center of the sphere. Therefore, $r_1 = r_2 = r$, is

$$\Delta \mathcal{P}_S = \frac{2\sigma}{r}.$$

(35)

In the case of the surface of a bubble, when the film limits this surface, an increment of surface pressure $\Delta \mathcal{P}_S$ serves as the continuous function on the film surface because choosing the positive side of the film unambiguously sets a positive side of a surface in its rather close points of proximity. Nevertheless, during the relatively long the turbulent condition of the dispersion system, there is an average size of the phase interface S.

In addition, it should be noted that the key parameter that characterizes the efficiency of the formation of a dispersion system is not the volume of the internal chamber of the chemical reactor, but the total area of the phase interface S, which is a function of the size of the chemical reactor.

In the equation (16), the constants a, b and k could be found experimentally. The algorithm of determining the sizes of a, b and k could be based on the simplest case: when $a = b$. The initial quantities of the processed components of the planned dispersion system are equal. It is easy to see that in this case the kinetic equation (16) can be written down as follows:

$$\frac{dv}{dt} = k \, (n_{a0} - x)^n .$$

(36)

In the kinetic equation (36), the quantities of the constants of the chemical processes k and n can be found by methods that are far beyond the scope of this work.

PROCESS OF GAS DISSOLUTION IN THE MODE OF TORSION-ORIENTED TURBULIZATION

Dissolution takes an important place in modern chemical technology. The basis of these processes is the ability of gases to interact with liquids to form solutions. The artificial saturation of oxygen by liquid is called an aeration. The artificial saturation of carbon dioxide is called a saturation and so on. The mechanism of the absorption is as follows: a boundary layer is formed on the gas–liquid interface, consisting of two layers adjacent to each other: one that consists of gas molecules and one that consists of liquid molecules. It should be noted the gas–liquid layer resists the passage of gas from the dispersed phase to the dispersion medium.

It is quite obvious that the gas dissolution process by liquid in the mode of torsion-oriented turbulization is caused by an intensive agitation processing mixture and leads to a substantial increase of the interface between gases and liquids. This allows new opportunities for the acceleration and optimization of the considered process. The use of torsion-oriented turbulization for absorption gases, lets us to consider the dissolution, for example, of the hazardous gas carbon dioxide CO_2 in water H_2O.

The solubility of gas in liquid is characterized by the coefficient of absorption $\propto$. That is, the coefficient of absorption $\propto$ is the amount of the volume of a gas that could be absorbed by one volume of liquid under the pressure of gas and vapors of a water of 101.3 kN/m² (that is equal 760 mm of Hg.) and with a temperature of 0 °C:

$$\propto = \frac{v_g}{v_\ell},$$

where v_g is the volume of gas, [m³]; and v_ℓ is the volume of solvent, [m³].

Thus, the solubility of gas in water can be characterized, by the amount of gas (in grams) that could be dissolved in 100 grams of water under the pressure of the gas and vapors of water of 101.3 kN/m².

The interacting of the carbon dioxide CO_2 with water H_2O, forms a coal acid H_2CO_3 that is dissociated with ions of a carbonate and bicarbonate: $\rightleftarrows$

$$H_2O + CO_2 \rightleftarrows H_2CO_3 \rightleftarrows$$
$$\rightleftarrows H^+ + HCO_3 \rightleftarrows 2\,H^+ + CO_3^{2-}.$$

The private coefficients of the speed of absorption for a gas dispersion phase and solvent (the dispersive environment) are set by the criteria of equations [36]:

$$K_G = f_1\,\frac{D_G}{d}\,Re_G^k\,Pr_G^l\left(\frac{d}{h}\right)^m;$$

$$K_L = f_2\,\frac{D_L}{d}\,Re_L^n\,Pr_L^p\left(\frac{d}{h}\right)^q;$$

For the subject process, the equation for the general coefficient of speed of absorption K [Kg/m² x hour x mm of Hg] [36] is as the follows:

$$K =$$

$$= \frac{1}{f_1 \frac{D_G}{d} \, Re_G^k \, Pr_G^l \, (\frac{d}{h})^m \cdot \frac{3600M}{22.4 \cdot 760} + f_2 \frac{D_L}{d} \, Re_L^n \, Pr_L^p \, (\frac{d}{h})^q \cdot \frac{3600\mathcal{H}}{760}}$$

or

$$K =$$

$$\frac{1}{0.211 \cdot f_1 \frac{D_G}{d} \, Re_G^k \, Pr_G^l \, (\frac{d}{h})^m \cdot M + 4.73 \cdot f_2 \frac{D_L}{d} \, Re_L^n \, Pr_L^p \, (\frac{d}{h})^q \cdot \mathcal{H}}$$

Where:

- f_1 and f_2 are amounts, that have to be determined.

- $k, l, m, n, p,$ and q are exponents of criteria of similarity,

- M is the molecular mass of the dissolved gas,

- $\mathcal{H}$ is the Henry's constant, [kg/m² x atmospheric pressure].

- Re_G is the Reynolds number for gas $(Re_G = \frac{dw_G}{v_G})$.

- Re_L is the Reynolds number for liquid $(Re_L = \frac{dw_L}{v_L})$.

- Pr_G is the Prandtl's number for gas $(Pr_G = \frac{v_G}{D_G})$.

- Pr_L is the Prandtl's number for liquid $(Pr_L = \frac{v_L}{D_L})$.

- D_G is the coefficient of diffusion for gas, [m²/s].

- D_L is the coefficient of diffusion for liquid, [m²/s].

- d is the internal diameter of the reactor, [m].

- h is the reactor's height, [m].

- v_G is the kinematic viscosity of gas (disperse phase), [m²/s].

- v_L is the kinematic viscosity of liquid (dispersive phase), [m²/s].

In compliance with Henry's Law, the dependence of the solubility of the gas in a specific liquid at a constant temperature is directly proportional to the pressure of this gas above the solution. It has to be understood that this law is suitable only for ideal solutions and with relatively low pressure. The Henry's Law can be expressed as

$$C = \mathcal{H}\, P \,,$$

where C is the molar concentration of gas in the solution; P is the partial pressure of gas over the solution; and $\mathcal{H}$ is the Henry's constant, which depends on the physical and mechanical properties of gas, solution and temperature.

1. Determination of the Coefficient k

It is necessary to experimentally determine the general coefficients of the speed of absorption k at the variable amount of the Re_G.

$$\text{For } Re_{G1}: \quad K_1 = \cfrac{1}{\cfrac{A}{Re_{G1}^{k}} + \cfrac{1}{K_L}};$$

$$\text{For } Re_{G2}: \quad K1 = \cfrac{1}{\cfrac{A}{Re_{G2}^{k}} + \cfrac{1}{K_L}};$$

$$\text{For } Re_{G3}: \quad K1 = \cfrac{1}{\cfrac{A}{Re_{G3}^{k}} + \cfrac{1}{K_L}},$$

where

$$A = \frac{1}{0.211 \cdot f_1 \frac{D_G}{d} Re_G^k \, Pr_G^l \, (\frac{d}{h})^m \cdot M}.$$

Thus, there are three equations with three unknowns: A, k and $\frac{1}{K_L}$. At the joint solution of these equations, k could be defined by the following equation:

$$(\alpha^k - 1) = B(1 - \beta^k),$$

where

$$\alpha = \frac{Re_{G2}}{Re_{G1}}, \quad \beta = \frac{Re_{G3}}{Re_{G1}} \quad \text{and} \quad B = \frac{\frac{1}{K_1} - \frac{1}{K_2}}{\frac{1}{K_2} - \frac{1}{K_3}}.$$

The amounts A and $\frac{1}{K_L}$ are the follows:

$$A = \frac{\frac{1}{K_1} - \frac{1}{K_2}}{\frac{2}{Re_{G1}^k} - \frac{1}{Re_{G2}^k}} \quad \text{and} \quad \frac{1}{K_L} = \frac{1}{K_1} - \frac{A}{Re_{G1}^k}.$$

2. Determination of the Coefficient m

Let us define the general coefficient of the speed of absorption K at the variable values $\frac{d}{h}$. Because the amount of A depends upon $\frac{d}{h}$, it is necessary for each of the values of $\frac{d}{h}$ to find A from the three values of K. Let us assume that $(\frac{d}{h})_1$ and $(\frac{d}{h})_2$ correspond to A_1 and A_2. Then

$$A_1 = \frac{1}{0.211 \cdot f_1 \frac{D_G}{d} Re_G^k \, Pr_G^l \, (\frac{d}{h})_1^m \cdot M},$$

$$A_2 = \frac{1}{0.211 \cdot f_2 \frac{D_G}{d} Re_G^k \, Pr_G^l \, (\frac{d}{h})_2^m \cdot M}.$$

To construct the ratio $\frac{A_1}{A_2}$, let us take the logarithm and definition from the equation received at the same time m:

$$m = \frac{\lg\frac{A_1}{A_2}}{\lg\frac{h_1}{h_2}} .$$

3. Determination of the Coefficient l

In this case K is defined at variable amount Pr, which can be received by testing the other gases. However, it is not only Pr that changes M and D_G are changing also. The amount of A depends upon Pr_G, therefore it is necessary for various gases to determine A from three values of K. Let us assume that for the gas, for which Pr_1, D_{G1}, and M_1 are known, the amount A_1 has been found. For the other gas for which Pr_2, D_{G2}, and M_2 are known, the amount A_1 is also found. Thus

$$A_1 = \frac{1}{0.211 \cdot f_1 \ \frac{D_{G1}}{d} \ Pr_{G1}^l \ \left(\frac{d}{h}\right)^m \cdot M_1} ;$$

$$A_2 = \frac{1}{0.211 \cdot f_2 \ \frac{D_{G2}}{d} \ Pr_{G2}^l \ \left(\frac{d}{h}\right)^m \cdot M_2} .$$

from where:

$$l = \frac{\lg \ \frac{A_1}{A_2} \ \frac{M_1}{M_2} \ \frac{D_{G1}}{D_{G2}}}{\lg\frac{Pr \ G2}{Pr \ G1}} .$$

4. Determination of the Coefficient f_1

If coefficients l and m are known, then the value of the f_1 function is easy to define from the equation:

$$f_1 = \frac{1}{0.211 \cdot A \ D_G \ Pr_G^l \ \left(\frac{d}{h}\right)^m \cdot M} ,$$

where A is the average value of this amount because coefficients k, l and m are calculated upon several values of A.

5. Determination of the Coefficient n

The amount K is at the variable amounts of Re_G, meaning that K is under a condition in which the frequency of the vibration approaches the frequency of the natural fluctuations of the components of the processed dispersion system. As a result, the quantity of vapor-gas bubbles increases, and we have the following equations:

$$\text{For } \boldsymbol{Re}_{G1}: K_1 = \frac{1}{\frac{1}{K_G} + \frac{E}{Re_{G1}^n}} \; ;$$

$$\text{For } \boldsymbol{Re}_{G2}: K_1 = \frac{1}{\frac{1}{K_G} + \frac{E}{Re_{G2}^n}} \; ;$$

$$\text{For } \boldsymbol{Re}_{G3}: K_1 = \frac{1}{\frac{1}{K_G} + \frac{E}{Re_{G3}^n}} \; ;$$

where

$$E = \frac{1}{4.73 \cdot f_2 \, \frac{D_L}{d} \, \boldsymbol{Pr}_L \, (\frac{d}{h})^q \cdot H} \; .$$

The exponent n, when solving these equations, is determined from the equality below:

$$(\alpha^n - 1) = z \, (1 - \beta^n)$$

where

$$\alpha = \frac{\boldsymbol{Re}_{G2}}{\boldsymbol{Re}_{G1}} \; ; \quad \beta = \frac{\boldsymbol{Re}_{G2}}{\boldsymbol{Re}_{G3}} \; ; \quad z = \frac{\frac{1}{K_1} - \frac{1}{K_2}}{\frac{1}{K_2} - \frac{1}{K_3}} \; .$$

This amounts to the following:

$$E = \frac{\frac{1}{K_1} - \frac{1}{K_2}}{\frac{2}{Re_{G1}^n} - \frac{1}{Re_{G2}^n}} \quad \text{and} \quad \frac{1}{K_G} = \frac{1}{K_1} - \frac{A}{Re_{G1}^n}.$$

6. Definition of the Exponent p

In this case, the variable amount is Pr_L. At the same time with Pr_L which changes when the other gas is in use, the amounts D_L and Henry's constant $\mathcal{H}$ are changing as well. So

$$P = \frac{\lg \frac{E_1}{E_2} \frac{\mathcal{H}_1}{\mathcal{H}_2} \frac{D_{G1}}{D_{G2}}}{\lg \frac{Pr_{G2}}{Pr_{G1}}}.$$

7. Definition of the Function f_2

In the presence of the known exponents p and q, this function is defined as:

$$q = \frac{1}{4.73 \cdot D_L \, Pr_G^p \, (\frac{d}{h})^q \cdot HE}.$$

Applying a method from [36], developed during the study of the processes of the dissolution of NH_3, SO_2, and HCl in a mixture with air in water, after mathematical processing, confirmed by experimental data, the following values were also obtained for the coefficients of the absorption rate, which can be used in the calculations in relation to this process:

$$K_G = 0.044 \, \frac{D_G}{d} \, Re_G^{0.752} \, Pr_G^{0.620} \, (\frac{d}{h})^{0.066}, \, [\text{M/s}]$$

$$K_L = 471 \frac{D_L}{d} \, Re_L^{0.324} \, Pr_L^{0.165} \, (\frac{d}{h})^{0.503}, \, [\text{M/s}]$$

CONCLUSION

For the practical use of the torsion-oriented turbulization phenomenon in physicochemical technology, it is necessary to conduct studies of the development of the fields of internal tension(s); the influence of the external revolting forces, the vibration impact on the development of the capillary-surface forces, and the forces of intermolecular interaction that develop in the course of the dissolution of hazardous and toxic gases and the formation of dispersion systems in batch and continuous modes.

REFERENCES

1. L. Amusin. Title: System and Method for Processing Dispersed Systems. United States Patent Application Publication. US 2015/0217244 A1. August 6, 2015.

2. L. Amusin. Title: System and Method for Processing Dispersed Systems. International Application Published Under The Patent Cooperation Treaty (PCT). International Publication Number WO 2015/119652 A1. August 13, 2015.

3. L. Amusin. Title: Method of Processing Molten Metals and Alloys. United States Patent Application Publication. US 2016/0040936 A1. February 11, 2016.

4. Л. Амусин. Теоретические основы физико-химической динамики процесса формирования дисперсных систем в режимах вибрационной кавитации и резонансной турбулентности. Израиль. Июнь, 27, 2019.
http://www.elektron2000.com/article/2206.html
L. Amusin. The Theoretical Base of Physicochmical Dynamics of the Process Formation Dispersion System in the Mode of Vibratory Cavitation and Resonance Turbulization. Israel, June 27, 2019,
http://www.elektron2000.com/article/2206.html

5. L. Amusin. Physicochemical Dynamics of Vibratory Cavitation and Resonance Turbulization Phenomena. Los Angeles, 2020. / ISBN: 978-64871-241-8

6. L. Amusin. Title: Process of Prevention of Hazardous and Toxic Gases Emission. Provisional Patent Application: US 63/372,992, Dated April 19, 2022. US 2022

7. Л.Г. Амусин. Исследование механизма развития полей капиллярных давлений при высушивании коллоидных капиллярно-пористых тел с целью управления их структурно-механическими свойствами. Диссертация на соискание ученой степени к.т.н. Калининский Политехнический институт. Калинин. 1976.

(L.Amusin. *Research of the Mechanism of the Development of Capillary Pressure Fields during Sorption of Colloidal Capillary-Porous Substances in order to control their structural and mechanical properties.* The Dissertation for the Ph.D. Doctorate. Kalinin Polytechnic University. City of Kalinin. Russia. 1976)

8. I.S. Pearsall. Cavitation. Mills and Boon Limited. London. 1972ю

9. А.Е. Акимов. Феноменологическое введение торсионных полей и их проявления в фундаментальных экспериментах. / В кн. «Горизонты науки и технологий XXI века», с.139-167.

10. Г.И. Шипов. Теория физического вакуума. М.: Наука,1997.

11. Е. С. Фрадкин. Избранные труды по теоретической физике. — М.: Наука, 2007

12. Д. М. Гитман, Е. С. Фрадкин, Ш. М. Шварцман. Квантовая электродинамика с нестабильным вакуумом. — М.: Наука, 1991

13. V. G. Bagrov, D. M. Gitman, A. S. Pereira, "Coherent and semiclassical states of a free particle", Phys. Usp., 57:9 (2014), 891–896

14. V. G. Bagrov, B. F. Samsonov, "Darboux transformation, factorization, supersymmetry in one-dimensional quantum mechanics", Theoret. and Math. Phys., 104:2 (1995), 1051–1060

15. V. G. Bagrov, V. V. Belov, M. F. Kondrat'eva, "The semiclassical approximation in quantum mechanics. A new approach", Theoret. and Math. Phys., 98:1 (1994), 34–38

16. D. Ivanenko, G. Sardanashvily The gauge treatment of gravity, Physics Reports 94 (1983) 1-45.

17. I. L. Buchbinder, S. D. Odintsov, I. L. Shapiro Effective Action in Quantum Gravity. CRC Press, 1992.

18. I. L. Buchbinder, S. M. Kuzenko Ideas_and_Methods_of Supersymmetry and Supergravity. — Bristol and Philadelphia: Institute of Physics Publishing, 1995.

19. I. L. Buchbinder, S. M. Kuzenko Ideas_and_Methods_of Supersymmetry_and_Supergravity. — второе издание, исправленное и дополненное. CRC Press, 1998.

20. D.I. Radin, R.D. Nelson. Evidence for conscious-related anomalies in random physical systems. Found. Phys., V.19, N12, 1989, p.1499-1514.

21. A.H. Jafary-AsL, S.N. Solanky, E. Aarcholt, C.W. Smith. Dielectric measurements on live biological material under magnetic resonance condition. J.Biol.Phys., 1983, v.11, p.15-22

22. H. Hayasaka, S. Takeuchi. Phys.Rev.Lett., 1989, v.63, N25, p.2701.

23. S. Imoushi, et all. J.Phys.Soc.Jap., 1991, v.60, N4, p.1150-1152.

24. V. de Sabbata, C. Sivaram. Fifth force as a manifestation of torsion. Int. J.Theor. Phys., 1990, v.29, N1, p.1-6.

25. V. de Sabbata, C. Sivaram. Strong spin-torsion interaction between spinning protons. Nuovo Cimento, 1989, V.101A, N2, p.273-283.

26. Физический Энциклопедический Словарь. Том 1. ГНИ «Советская Энциклопедия». Москва. 1960

27. Ю.Б. Румер, М.Ш. Рывкин. Термодинамика, Статистическая Физика и Кинетика. Издание 2, Москва. 1977.

28. В.А. Эткин. Об ориентационном взаимодействии. (http://zhurnal.lib.ru), 05-22-2005.

29. В.А. Эткин. К термодинамике ориентируемых систем. (http://zhurnal.lib.ru), 07-10-2005.

30. C. De Groom. П. Мазур. Неравновесная термодинамика. Москва. Мир. 1958.

31. Физический Энциклопедический Словарь. Том 3. ГНИ «Советская Энциклопедия». Москва. 1960

32. В.А. Эткин. Торсионно-ориентационные процессы. Материалы международной научной конференции. Хоста. Сочи. 25-29 Август, 2009.

33. В.А. Эткин. Термокинетика. ТПИ. Тольятти. 1999.

34. В.А. Эткин. Энергодинамика. С-Пб. Наука. 2008.

35. G. Korn, T. Korn. Mathematical Handbook for Scientists and Engineers. Dover Publications, Inc. Mineola. New York. 2016.

36. М.Д. Кузнецов. Определение коэффициентов скорости абсорбции по методу подобия. Журнал Прикладной Химии № 1, Москва. 1948

Printed in the United States
by Baker & Taylor Publisher Services